BUTTERFLIES ARE OUR FRIENDS

A fresh approach to helping
children with anxiety and fears

Written by Nicola Farr, PhD
Illustrated by Hannah Broadway

Edited by Lynn Hess

To the three brightest lights I am blessed to know,

my children;

Joshua, Emilia and Reuben.

Contents

Advanced Praise

"Butterflies Are Our Friends is a clear, simple, colorful little book with a deeply profound and important message: You are well, by nature, despite what you feel. So are your children. Our feelings are not problems, but superpowers. This book can radically improve the way you experience life and how you support your children. Please, read it and then share it with others!"

Amy Johnson, Ph.D., author of *The Little Book of Big Change* and creator of The Little School of Big Change

"The message in this ground-breaking book is simple but very powerful indeed. It will help many parents supporting anxious children as it is written from the author's deep understanding of the issues from a personal, parenting and professional perspective. It is no ordinary parenting book. The underlying principles Nicola is sharing here have the potential to transform the readers' understanding and experience of life. This beautiful work marks a paradigm shift in parenting books."

Carol Boroughs, Three Principles facilitator and mentor

"This book. If every parent every where could read and embody what Dr. Nicola has written about, we would change the world. Your child is not broken. Nothing needs fixing. Your child is serving as a wonderful mirror, showing you a manifestation of your own inner world so that you might have a brilliant opportunity to grow yourself, and then, step in with wisdom and nurturing power to grow them. The conceptual foundation of such a shift can be hard to grasp. But Dr. Nicola's book makes it understandable and immediately approachable. I've never read anything like it and I want to tell the whole world about it!"

Vanessa Lapointe, Ph.D., registered psychologist, parenting educator, and mom

"In this beautifully illustrated and easy to read book lies a secret to true freedom. In many ways, we are trapped in the world of our thoughts and Nicola shows us a simple path to liberation.

Having been a parent coach for many years, and also doing workshops in prisons, the wisdom that is shared in this book reflects my experience exactly.

That we human beings are fundamentally perfect and free and we can access that freedom at any time. Applying this understanding to ourselves and to our interactions with our children can revolutionize the way we parent and contribute to a great positive shift in our world. Thank you for writing this book Nicola, I know it's going to deeply affect many lives as it already has mine."

Vivek Patel, conscious parenting educator and founder of Meaningful Ideas

"A refreshing, clear, easy to understand and follow book I highly recommend. Nicola has captured the essence through which we all experience life, with its ups and downs, and explains in a uniquely touching and thought-provoking way how to explore this, either with your children or by yourself. For children and parents who are struggling this book shines hope into the darkness and while not a "fixing" book, is certainly a book that can trigger huge insights and change lives. I certainly will be using this fantastic resource in my work in schools, with children and parents with full confidence it will have huge impact time after time."

Julie Smith, certified child and parent coach and co-founder of My Mental Health Rocks campaign

"Nicola presents an uncomplicated and profound understanding of how we experience life, which not only can transform our children's relationships with fear and anxiety, but also nurture our whole family's relationship with suffering towards freedom. The practical examples help parents make an immediate impact, and this gem of a book is a highly recommended read for any parent wanting to help their children live their most joyous loving life."

Phil Goddard, Relationship Coach

"There is perhaps no greater job than parenting--and especially parenting our children through bouts of anxiety and stress without becoming anxious and stressed out ourselves! With gentle words and beautiful illustrations not normally produced for adults and 'grown up' books, Nicola Farr has written a simple, yet profound book that will soothe parents and, through them, their children. This is the beginning of true peace and lasting mental health for current and future generations. I cannot think of a greater gift to give the world. Thank you, Nicola!"

Ami Chen Mills-Naim, author of *The Spark Inside: A Special Book for Youth* and *State of Mind in the Classroom: Thought, Consciousness and the Essential Curriculum for Healthy Learning*, Founder, Ami Chen Coaching and Education

"The knowledge and personal story that Nicola shares in this gorgeous little book is information that will help parents and children create a beautiful relationship of understanding with each other. Its core message is brought to life through Nicola's words and beautiful colour illustrations, that make it a joy to read. It's an absolute gem of a book that every family should have in their home."

Katie Foster, virtual assistant and founder of Destination Freedom

Beautifully written and illustrated, Nicola captured my heart with this simple and yet powerful message. There are many books available based on the teachings of Syd Banks but this is the first that I have had the privilege of reading that speaks directly to parents, gently pointing them to the miracles within themselves and their children to gain a different perspective. I wish I could have read this when my children were younger, I am sure I would have 'tried' less often to be a good parent and instead allowed myself to be the kind and loving parent I was always trying to be.

When considering what I love the most about Nicola's book, it was this: In a world where we are surrounded by resources teaching us how to manage a child's behavior, their fears and anxieties, it is wonderful to discover that we all have the capacity within us, to return to peace, love and understanding. We all have the light that Nicola so powerfully shows us and that when we find our own, it allows our children to be guided to find their own light.

Thank you Nicola, for being a ray of light to so many.

Nicky Bartley, transformation coach & trainer

"If you want to connect with your children and help them see they are not their insecure and stressful thinking then this book is for you. Discover the simplicity of looking beyond fear-based stories to the deeper resilience and resourcefulness within young people. Nicola's wise words are accompanied by beautiful illustrations. This is a reassuring and practical guide for parents."

Liz Scott, co-founder of innercompassguide.com

Preface

Once upon a time there was a beautiful, happy little girl born into this world. Although she didn't know it, this little girl had a superpower.

For many years nobody else realised it either. In fact, both the little girl and the people around her thought it was a curse rather than a blessing, and they tried many things to get rid of it. When these didn't work, the little girl was sad. She came to believe there was something so wrong and broken in her that she would never be fixed.

She loved other people and other children with all her heart and longed to be loved back. But from a young age she felt lonely and different from other children, and always felt worried they'd discover her faultiness and realise she was strange and broken. Even her adored older brother didn't seem to like her much and was frequently mean and unkind.

One day she moved to a new school and was happy to discover that one of the few friends she had from her old school had also moved there. But the friend was ashamed to admit they were friends—she pretended not to know the little girl and ignored her when she tried to speak or play with her.

This broke the little girl's heart. She thought her friend had discovered her secret and knew that she was odd and broken. She felt deeply ashamed and lonely. She became even more convinced that she wasn't good enough to be anyone's friend; she wasn't nice enough to deserve friends.

The feeling of rejection was intense

and unbearable, and the little girl didn't think her heart could stand it happening again. She became terrified of talking to people and stopped smiling and looking people in the eye. She became lonelier and lonelier and felt weirder and weirder. Soon she forgot how to even make or be a friend and she began to dread going to school.

Worrying about school and being by herself and having no friends became all-consuming. Some nights she would be so anxious she hardly slept. Some days at school she would be so fearful she would hide in the toilets or in the school garden.

She felt embarrassed and ashamed to be so weak and pathetic. And she didn't want to upset or disappoint the grown-ups in her life, so she never told anyone.

The weight of this felt all-encompassing. She could barely concentrate on lessons or learning; her head was too full of fears and imaginings, dread and shame.

Her anxiety grew so much that she would physically shake and feel sick at the idea of meeting new people, and the thought of talking in front of her class caused extreme panic. She found many strategies to avoid stressful things like this and became adept at excuses and get-out ploys. When she did have to face any kind of public speaking or performance her heart raced so much that she couldn't think, and she often thought she would pass out.

This anxiety continued into adulthood. It flared up and receded at different points, but was always a huge part of her life, a huge barrier to living freely and authentically. She found many other vices to help push the pain away—including the eating disorder bulimia, which greatly impacted her wellbeing from her mid teens until her late twenties.

Many years later, this little girl would grow up to learn that behind ALL of this upset and stress was her innocently missed superpower. She would discover that all along there had been nothing wrong with her, she wasn't broken, and she'd never needed fixing.

Her superpower was that her body's alarm system was EXTRA responsive. It picked up IMMEDIATELY if she wasn't feeling safe or if the people around her were inauthentic, or if she was off-track and not in alignment with her core peace and wellbeing. Her hands and feet would start pouring sweat at the smallest fearful or anxious thought. If something felt too much or too scary, her mind and body would respond instantly.

And what this little girl didn't know (and neither did the adults in her life) was that this bodily response was her FRIEND, that it was a perfectly designed signal to guide her back to safety and peace.

It took this little girl nearly 35 years to discover this secret. When she did, she felt the happiest she'd been in forever. And she was determined to help other children and other grown-ups learn about this superpower and teach them about feelings and anxiety so that fewer people would have to suffer like she had.

How do I know all of this so intimately?
Because that little girl was, of course, me.
And this book represents the gift of understanding and hope that I wish I'd been given myself.

15

How to use this book

From many years of working with parents, plus my own experience of raising three little ones, I know that seeing our children distressed or suffering is, without doubt, one of THE hardest aspects of this precious role we get to undertake. Quite understandably, our instinct is to jump in and get rid of the pain, make things better, get them 'fixed' in any way we possibly can.

We turn to books, websites, professionals, ANYONE, to give us solutions, strategies, or techniques that might do this. We take our children to every kind of specialist we come across that we sense may know something we don't, or offer the cure and hope we're searching for.

And there is no shortage of such resources—every where we look we can find a multitude of options, and if it's opinions and diagnoses we are seeking, we will not struggle to gather them.

The approach I share though, both in this book and my coaching practise, offers a very different focus. I have come to see that it is usually far more helpful to take our attention *away* from specific diagnoses and symptoms and *away* from scrutinising our children.

And to look first instead at deepening our own understanding of how experience is created and towards a much broader perspective about how life works.

I am not ruling out the need or usefulness of ever working directly with children. But what I do believe is that, where possible, this is not the first step. The first step is always to look inwards, within *ourselves* as parents, to how we're navigating life and showing up for our children.

Because what I've seen so very clearly, countless times now, is that parental personal transformation has a direct and hugely positive impact on our children. The hard to hear truth is that when *we* change and when *we* really get grounded in understanding the nature of our miraculous humanness, many of our children's 'issues' or 'problems' naturally fall away.

Perhaps this sounds too good to be true? I know what you mean, I would possibly have said the same not that long ago. And yet, every single day I am so grateful to have this new perspective, it has changed my life and parenting indescribably for the better.

So I invite you to simply stay open to hearing something new—and to also consider that you've been brought to this book for a reason; the fact that you are reading these words right now looks to me to be absolutely no accident.

But if you were hoping for a 'how to' guide, a book with step-by-step solutions to get rid of anxious feelings for good (in you or your child), I'm afraid this is not that. And if you're tempted to skip straight to the "How to help your child with anxiety" section, please don't; it will likely make very little sense. "Butterflies are our Friends" has been written with the explicit intention of being read all the way through, and the first part *directly* informs and clarifies the more practical aspects and examples of the second part.

The good news, though, is that because what's shared here is not a prescription or 'how-to' formula, you have my full permission to switch off your intellectual hat and to read from a soft place of heart and open curiosity. There is no need to struggle to grasp concepts or strive to understand; this never takes us in a helpful direction. You can trust that you will hear and take from this exactly what you need right now, without any undue effort. And if something happens to land with you or resonate, please know it's because it's stirring a re-remembrance of what you already know deep down to be true. And that is just perfect, because it's only from this place anyway that deep and lasting change can unfold.

This book would not exist if it were not for the insights of Sydney Banks, a Scottish welder who had a sudden enlightenment experience in 1973 and devoted his life to sharing what he saw. All the metaphors and analogies shared here have come directly or indirectly from the many teachers and coaches who have continued to share this understanding with people all over the world since he died in 2009. (See Resources, page 65)

Who are we?

No matter who we are, what we look like, or the circumstances we are born into, we humans all have the same potential within us to lead a joyful, fulfilling life.

Some days this is very obvious to us. We feel calm and content and settled. The things we want to do get done effortlessly, we feel in flow and at ease, and connection and love for others is natural and uncomplicated.

Other days, not so much. We feel like life is overwhelmingly hard, our heart feels heavy, restless, fed up, cranky, and scared, and we conclude that we are just NOT ENOUGH.

If we don't understand why this is, we can feel a bit rocked, a bit Jekyll and Hyde-like and confused as to who is the 'real' us.

And here's one of THE most important messages of this book:

the REAL you is the peaceful, at ease, loving version.

How do I know? Because this is who we ALL are. Underneath all the external differences, circumstances, and personal thinking, we are all made of the same stuff, all part of the extraordinary, unexplainable energy of the universe.

Call it Divine Intelligence, God, Creator, Mind, Energy, Chi, Tao, Innate Wisdom, Bananas, whatever you like. But you don't have to look very far to see that there is SOMETHING much greater than us that is opening the flowers, healing our bodies, and making and growing our babies. There is something within us all that is guiding us constantly, a voice of wisdom and clarity that is pointing us to the next right decision or best step.

And that something has a power and mystery that we can only marvel at—but that we can't take even the slightest credit or ownership for.

I call it lots of things, but a particular favourite is 'light'. For me, it speaks to a visual glow and vitality that I can see and sense in others, and a feeling of flow and lightheartedness that helps me recognise in myself when I'm in touch with that place inside me that is connected to this light.

In this light, this spark within, is all the wisdom, love, resilience, peace, and joy we need for our time on this planet. It's operating for us and within us whether we are aware of it or not. But when we do realise and start to trust in it, this is where true magic can start to happen.

What is thought?

LIFE

If we could all be in touch with this loving,

perfect part of ourselves 24/7,

life would be a piece of cake.

But the fact is, it would also be a bit dull.

What makes humans so fantastically

rainbow-coloured and human is that we have the

capacity to create a huge variety of experience here on this planet.

We have the gift of thought coming through us.

And the first important thing to know about thought . . . which was a

very NEW idea to me until recently . . . is that thought and feeling are

directly related.

In order to experience a feeling, we have to have a thought first. And

similarly, when we think, there is always a related experiential feeling

that we sense in our physical form.

Thought is not occurring over

here while feelings are arising

separately or randomly over there.

Thoughts
Feelings

Nope, thought and feeling are a pair—they're the opposite sides of the same coin.

Thoughts

Feelings

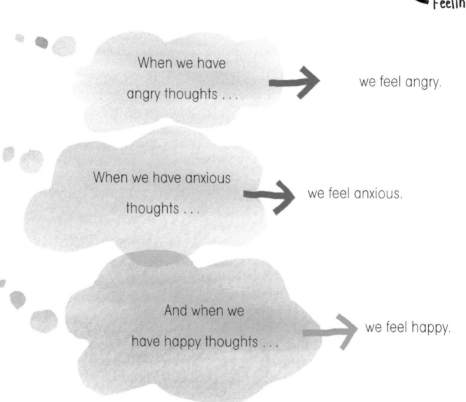

When we have angry thoughts . . . → we feel angry.

When we have anxious thoughts . . . → we feel anxious.

And when we have happy thoughts . . . → we feel happy.

What's crucial about understanding this is that it forces us to recognise that **our experience is created internally; NOTHING outside of us can MAKE us feel a certain way.**

Even though (I know, I know) it DEFINITELY often looks like it.

So, you know that traffic jam, millionth toddler juice spillage, rude boss, bad weather, empty bank account...? None of these are CAUSING us to feel grumpy or frustrated or upset. It's our THINKING about them, the specific nature of our thoughts about these things, that is resulting in us feeling this grumpiness.

Let's take the toddler and the juice for example. Tell me, honestly, is it not the case that your reaction to the same type of spillage (you know that one that happens every meal time, just as you've finally served up and sat down) varies considerably? Some days, you are Zen and calm ('Oopsie, let me help you clean that up!'), some days you sigh internally and roll your eyes, other days you can't help but let out an exasperated 'Oh for f@#* sake, Daisy Bee, have you really spilt it yet again??!'—and every variation of reaction in between.

But Daisy Bee has not changed, and neither has the spillage. It's only your thinking about the spillage that has changed. And in a low mood and busy state of mind your thinking about this incident is likely very different from when you're in a high mood and calm state of mind.

It's as though the thoughts give us different glasses, and things look incredibly different depending on the type of glasses we have on in that moment.

And this thought/feeling relationship is a FACT, a universal law, just as gravity is. And if feelings always come from thinking, this HAS to be the case 100% of the time whether we realise it or not:

When I use the word 'thought' here, I'm not referring to personal thought or thinking in the way it's usually described, to mean deciding or choosing or working out a problem or solution. I'm referring to thought as a more mysterious gift, an unexplainable creative energy that shows up through us, a stream of ideas that appears to arrive in our minds from no immediately obvious source—some have called this universal thought.

Please keep reading even if that feels a bit what the heck-ish. It's a fairly new way of looking at things, so I know it might sound a little odd or puzzling at first. But this way of understanding how our mind works is changing people's lives rapidly, and I'd love for you (and your children) to have the chance to be similarly impacted.

And also keep reading because . . . well, haven't you had this experience yourself? As in, you've been minding your own business doing the laundry or having a shower and you suddenly have an awesome idea or breakthrough or realisation. Something you didn't consciously choose or decide to put there and couldn't possibly have 'thought up' if you tried. That's you settling down enough to hear or give space to universal thought coming through you, or arising within you.

And it seems to be the case that this is what is going on within us MUCH more than we usually realise. All the time, in fact.

A helpful way to view this thinking is like a continuous ticker tape coming into our head, consistently spitting out new thoughts. If we just allow it as though we are sitting back and observing this stream of thoughts, it keeps ticking on, pushing out the previous thoughts by replacing them with new ones.

What we're not usually told is that **none of these thoughts are directly related to us or personal to us. They are not telling us anything REAL about who we are. They are not OURS.**

If the thought is 'You are a green-eared, purple-nosed baboon', we find this pretty easy to disbelieve. This information does not feel in any way in alignment with our experience of ourselves and we have certainty that it's not true. We might notice it, even laugh at it, but then pretty quickly let it go and allow other thoughts to naturally take its place.

But if the thought is 'You are dumb and have no hope for the future', dismissing this thought as nothing we need to take seriously suddenly feels a lot harder. It doesn't feel like a big leap to assume that this could be true, and we can usually find lots of examples or 'evidence' to back it up—for example, failing or getting a low mark on a test, or not being able to do something straight away. **And because we humans have evolved (for survival and safety) to be more attuned to negativity, we are naturally biased towards attaching to these kinds of thoughts.**

But when we identify with 'You are dumb', we inadvertently give it more energy to stick around and become a habitual part of our inner dialogue. And, all too soon, it can feel a very real part of who we actually are.

It's as though we are putting our finger on the ticker tape, jamming it and preventing that thought from moving on—as well as temporarily blocking the flow of new, fresh thought from coming in.

Another nice visual way of describing this process is imagining a snow globe, where the fixed figurine at the bottom is who you really are, your light (or as some describe it, your 'inner diamond'), and each snowflake is a thought.

When we allow some of these snowflakes to disturb or agitate us more than others—they shake up our snow globe. By taking them personally or believing them to be meaningful, we inadvertently give them energy and prevent them from naturally settling back to the ground. And when we worry about what each thought means and what's going to happen, and what we should do, all this personal thinking and ruminating is like continuing to shake the globe.

29

When our mind is white with snow like this, it covers up our innate wisdom and light—and it becomes virtually impossible to feel at peace or remember who we really are. But when we can rest in the understanding that NONE of this thinking needs to be taken seriously, that it doesn't say anything REAL about us, we naturally stop shaking the snow. We realise that there is nothing more we need to do than take our attention off the thoughts, and allow them to naturally melt away and disappear.

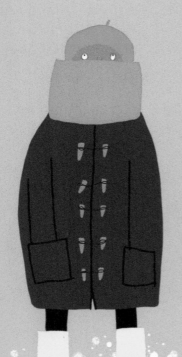

When we do, we glimpse our real self again. We feel light and at ease, with nothing churning or floating around in our mind. In this state, there is plenty of room for new ideas or fresh new thinking to come in. This is the place where we might come up with an inspired insight or solutions that might help us.

Imagine you are feeling a bit scared or anxious about starting a new activity you've never done before:

Thought:
I've never done this before; I don't like new things

Feeling:
scared and nervous

Thought (about the thought):
I'm scared and I hate being scared. It's because I'm shy
and I'm not good at making friends.

Feeling:
worried, anxious shy

Thought (about the thought about the thought):
I hate being shy! Why am I shy and everyone else isn't?

Feeling:
sadness, frustration, even more shy, more anxious

Thought (about the thought about the thought about the thought):
People won't like me if I'm shy. How can I stop myself from looking
shy? I need to hide it or they'll all hate me.

Feeling:
embarrassed, overwhelmed, more worried, more anxious

Thought (about the thought about the thought
about the thought about the thought):
That boy next to me didn't even look at me; he knows
I'm shy and he hates me already.

Feeling:
sad, lonely, rejected, ashamed, yet more anxious

31

Can you see how in this situation you're now walking around with layers upon layers of additional personal thinking that you've added to that one anxious thought that arrived in your mind? You're now carrying a layer cake fit for a Queen's worth of anxious thinking and angst, and it **all started because you BELIEVED that initial thought to be saying something true about you and who you really are.**

Why is an understanding of the nature of thought helpful?

Experiencing fear is a normal and helpful part of the human design—our fight/flight/freeze response evolved to be activated in  an emergency to keep us safe and to give us the temporary supply of adrenaline and resources necessary to save our lives in emergencies. In fact, we likely wouldn't be here at all if our ancestors hadn't had been fearful of being eaten by a tiger or eating poisonous berries.

The trouble is that the biological part of us, our brain, can't distinguish on its own what it needs to be truly fearful of, so it signals us to take seriously ALL of the anxious thinking that comes through us. It doesn't know that keeping us in this hyper-aroused state for long periods is both unnecessary and damaging. And when we don't know not to take our thinking so seriously, we inadvertently keep this thinking alive and experience it in our body—as well as innocently generating more of the same kind of thinking.

It is also now well-documented that staying in this stress response for prolonged periods (anything more than 30 minutes every 48–72 hours) results in physical responses like inflammatory reactions, hormone changes, and decreased immune functioning. This is our body's way of further signalling that we are not in our wellbeing and ease—**it is a helpful response designed to get us back on track.** When we don't know this, though, we can easily get caught up in a reactive cycle of MORE stressful thinking, which leads to even more physical symptoms and more thinking and so on. (See Bill Pettit's work in Resources for more on this). And as parents, if we don't deeply understand what's happening, these kinds of physical panic attacks can be particularly tough to witness in our children.

How and why particular types of thoughts show up in my mind but not in yours looks to be another part of the great mystery of the universe.

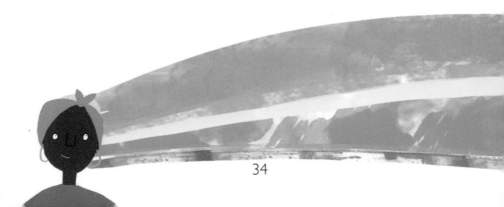

But it does seem as though some of us are predisposed to more of some types of thoughts than others.

If you imagine a rainbow of potential thoughts where every colour roughly represents a genre, it appears some of us are born with an extra big dose of potential anxious thoughts, others are more prone to fearful ones, others to depressed ones, and so on. **In other words, we all have a unique rainbow with colour bands of differing thicknesses.** And when our mind is stressed, this is the particular flavour of snow that is likely to be created and that we are therefore more susceptible to believing and taking seriously.

It also seems to be true that the extent to which we take our thinking seriously can be picked up from those around us. If our parents believed that the world is scary and not to be trusted, it makes sense that we would have been more likely to take this type of thinking seriously— and in doing so keep it sticking around and/or generate more of the same.

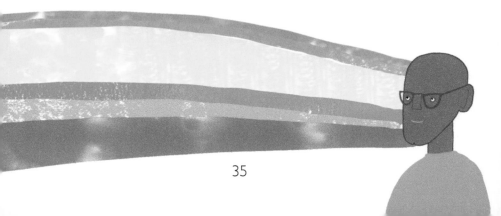

35

The reason we can experience and feel our thinking is because humans have the gift of consciousness; we are AWARE. Our thinking is translated into feelings via our bodily senses, to give a FELT physical three-dimensional experience. We are like the hot water that different flavour tea bags (thoughts) are dunked in. Each tea bag gives us a different flavour, a different experience. But if it wasn't for the water, we wouldn't be able to discern this.

Because this sensory experience is so vivid and strong, it can feel like a very urgent call to action; much of the time it absolutely doesn't feel like fleeting thought taking form and running through our sensory system. One of the reasons this thought/feeling connection is not immediately obvious is because it's much easier to recognise the bodily feelings and sensations than it is to catch many of the thoughts that continuously flit through our mind. The thought always comes first, but it's not necessarily easy to spot—and sometimes thoughts are pretty low-level or unconscious.

The feelings that arise are often much more noticeable. And sensations such as butterflies in our tummy can feel uncomfortable, almost as though there are real live butterflies fluttering inside of us. Indeed, sometimes they feel unbearable, especially the bodily symptoms of fear and anxiety: racing heart, shaking, violent pulse, clenched muscles, nausea, breathlessness, and many more.

But what we usually miss (because no one ever told us) is that **this information our body is giving us is HELPFUL. Butterflies are our FRIENDS.**

The butterflies (and other symptoms) arise to **remind us that we are off-track, that we are either cycling thoughts from the past or believing made-up, unsubstantiated ones about the future.** The feelings are letting us know that our thinking is NOT in alignment with who we really are.

But if it wasn't for the butterflies, we wouldn't know that the thoughts passing through shouldn't be believed, that we don't need to take them seriously. These bodily symptoms are simply warning signals, just as a rumble strip lets us know we are no longer driving centrally on the road and we're in danger of hitting the sides, and the receptors in our hands warn us to remove them to prevent more damage if we touch a hot stove.

When we can view anxiety and fearful thinking like this—as HELPFUL and as temporary and transient rather than as a fixed part of who we are—our whole approach to life shifts, including how we support our children.

How does all this help me with my anxious child?

Hopefully the KEY insight you can take away from this book is that you don't have an anxious child. But what you may well have, though, is a child who has anxious thinking, and in some cases, a LOT of anxious thinking.

Anxiety is **not** a fixed condition, a fixed part of who we ARE, an unchangeable, inevitable, it's-in-my-genes-and-there's-nothing-I-can-do-about-it condition.

No. Anxiety is a flavour of thinking that we get caught up in (for short or long periods) and that we BELIEVE to be telling us something real about who we really are.

Shyness and anxiety are temporary, transient—NOT a permanent part of who your child really is. **Your child is NOT his or her anxious thinking.**

The feeling or behaviour that is showing up for your child in any moment is a clue, a guide, a FRIEND. It is letting us know that your child has lost sight of who they are and is caught up in believing the

anxious thinking to be real and

genuinely scary and meaningful.

As we all do sometimes—or,

when we don't know

that this is how it works,

an awful lot!

If we can hold this perspective in our hearts, we show up differently. We see our kids from a place of compassion and love rather than fear. We are no longer worried about what's wrong with them or how they are going to cope, nor consumed with guilt about what we did wrong. **We UNDERSTAND that what's going on for them is exactly the same as what is going on for all humans.**

When all this thinking drops away, we find OURselves in a much calmer place, and much more in tune with our own light.As a result, it becomes much easier to intuitively know how to help our child and point them to their own resilience and light. We are more open to fresh ideas about how best to do this and to listen to our in-the-moment guidance.

One of my clients put it like this:

'The first thing I came to realise was that I wasn't an awful mum. The opposite, in fact—that I was the best mum for my children and that I had just temporarily forgotten this. Once I had seen this, this love, this resilience and innate goodness in myself, I started to see it in my children. Instead of projecting into the future and wondering if my son was going to end up in jail, I could see that when his behaviour became difficult, it meant he was feeling off-track. It didn't mean he was a bad person, it was just a warning signal to show he wasn't in a good place, he wasn't coming from his true self. This meant that I could have compassion for him. **I could do what I needed to do to keep him, myself, and my other children safe in that moment (take him out of the room, for example) but do it from a place of love and calm rather than anger and fear.**

In the past, I would have seen him as 'suffering with anxiety' and looked for ways to fix him. This led me to being anxious and impatient myself and being cross with him. If he woke in the night with fears of being alone, I would have kept putting him back to bed in an irritated and not-gentle fashion, quite possibly sharing some of my anxieties about the situation with him, such as, "You won't get enough sleep and will find it hard tomorrow unless you settle down".

I now don't believe he has or ever had anxiety. Sure, he has anxious thoughts from time to time, as we all do, but now I see they are just temporary energy passing through. They don't say anything about who he really is, and I can point him instead towards his resilience, his innate ability to cope, that he's always had and always will have. He's not broken as I once thought. There really is nothing to fix. And it's from seeing this and being able to point him towards it that his anxiety has dissolved and is simply no longer an issue.'

How to help a child caught up in a moment of anxious thinking

Feeling anxious or fearful can seemingly come out of the blue and take our kids (and us) by surprise, and we tend to immediately look for an external circumstance or thing to blame or identify as the 'cause' of these feelings.

But it's this misunderstanding that can innocently take us in the wrong direction when trying to help our kids. Because, in fact, the truth is that **anxious feelings come directly from anxious thinking**—and this anxious thinking can come through us at any time. We're not in control of the thoughts that pop into our heads, any more than we are in control of how our hair grows or our nails repair after a tear.

43

And once the thoughts are there and we're living in the feeling of them, we can't easily make them go away.

But what we can do is NOT TAKE THEM TOO SERIOUSLY and just know that they are temporary and that our child has momentarily lost touch with their true self and wellbeing.

HEAVY THOUGHTS

Not
Take
them
Too
Seriously

44

Because, as already discussed, our children's default setting is wellbeing and light. They will always naturally self-correct back to this state, and the less we get in their way or add to their thought-storm, the quicker this is likely to happen.

'Teaching' our kids—or anyone—more tools or 'stuff' to use in the moment tends to give them more to think about. And the more they're trying to think about, the more this focuses them ON their upsetting thinking, and the more likely they are to stay stuck there.

Similarly, it's usually best to not repeatedly ask them what's wrong or try to 'get to the bottom of it'. The exact content or source of the thought is not really the issue right now or a helpful thing to focus on. We do not need to get them to change their thinking (as other approaches sometimes suggest), but instead simply know that giving their thinking less energy will allow it to pass.

So, in the moment of anxiety, just acknowledging our child's feelings is enough. Sensing that we understand but are not anxious or stressed ourself allows them to get a glimpse that this is not a real emergency. This can be hard, I know, as it can be very distressing to watch our children suffer, and it is all too easy to join them in their upset.

It's also really important to remember that because our experience of reality is created internally, we can't MAKE or convince our kids into seeing what we're seeing. Our worldview or experience of reality is unique because of the unique glasses we are wearing. As much as it may be obvious to us that there are no snakes in our child's bed, it's probably not helpful or respectful to dismiss or invalidate their belief that there are. It can feel frustrating, annoying even, that they are so convinced of something that in your world is blatantly not happening, but trying to be as patient and understanding as you can is always going to be the best way to help them.

It can be helpful to recognise as well that **the goal is not to get rid of anxiety or expend energy trying to replace or cover up anxious thinking.** Anxiety does not have to be feared or vilified or viewed as an affliction or illness. And it's not something that can be driven out by force or by learning specific techniques for getting rid of it.

It's much more about being okay with the feelings that are showing up,

knowing they are made of the same energy as happiness and excitement and all other feelings, and not being in resistance to them. It's about remembering that the anxious feelings are a helpful reminder that our child is keeping their attention stuck on a particular flavour of thinking, and in doing so they are inadvertently creating an even bigger thought-storm. When we show up for our children from this place, they are able to sense and tune into this feeling too—even without us having to explicitly articulate it or say very much.

And from this perspective, there's very little in the moment that we need to DO. It's much more about giving them room to truly feel their feelings, and in doing so prevent a jam in the ticker tape and allow space for fresh thought to come in.

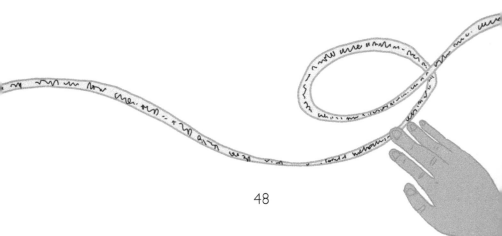

A common scenario with kids prone to anxious thinking is refusing at the last minute to go to a party or event, even when they know the people there well:

(NOTICE HOW STAYING IN OUR WELLBEING CAN HELP OUR CHILDREN ACCESS THEIR OWN MORE QUICKLY. WE DON'T HAVE TO EXPLICITLY TALK TO THEM ABOUT THE TRANSIENT AND IMPERSONAL NATURE OF THOUGHT OR 'TEACH' THEM ANYTHING—THE BIGGEST IMPACT AND LEARNING COMES FROM THE WAY *WE* SHOW UP AND RESPOND TO THEM WHEN THEY'RE STRUGGLING.)

Actions that might occur to you in this kind of situation could be things like sitting quietly with them, slowing down your breathing and thinking, consciously connecting to your light and inner calm, suggesting you go for a walk/out the room/do something else for a while (or whatever's appropriate), or quietly reminding them that they are safe, that you're going to stay with them and that this will pass. **The key here is that when YOU are settled down and not worried or fearful about your child's anxiety, you are much more likely to be able to access an intuitive knowing about the best way to help them in that moment.**

And probably the most effective way to increase the likelihood that you will remain in a place of wellbeing and ease is to do exactly what you are doing right now by reading this book; become deeply grounded in understanding what is happening, how our mind works, and what anxiety is and what it isn't. The more you can read, listen, and immerse yourself in this understanding, the more your trust and 'knowing' will become cemented (see Resources).

This is not a 'quick fix', I know—but I guarantee that doing so will positively affect the whole of YOUR life too, not just your children's.

51

Case Study

Eating breakfast the other morning, my 5-year-old suddenly screamed and dashed away crying from the table.

Amidst big sobs he said he wanted his pancakes but couldn't eat them because he was 'scared' of them.

Aware that they'd been cooked by Daddy (!) I checked for remains of fearsome monsters or deadly snakes, but there were no obvious traces.

I wasn't too far off the mark though—it turned out he'd suddenly imagined that there were spiders hidden inside and thought he had eaten one.

He said he KNEW they weren't real or really there but they FELT like they were and wouldn't get out of his head. It's the shadow side to his huge creativity and capacity to engage in imaginative play for hours—and it's tough, I think I would have been horrified too!

His outward behaviour looked irrational and it would have been easy to think he was being 'silly' or 'disobedient'. And I can see how quickly I could have despaired that he has a pancake 'phobia', never served him pancakes again for fear of upsetting him, and started looking into ways to get him 'cured'.

Instead, I did the same thing that works for all of us when we're caught up like this; very little. I calmly held him and stayed with him through his upset, just listening and holding onto the knowing that it would pass. I didn't mention the pancakes or encourage him to try eating them again. After a little while he stopped crying and started talking about something else. And five minutes later he was back eating his pancakes again.

Phrases NOT usually helpful to say:

Calm down

Stop crying/moaning/making such a fuss

Why are you being so silly, you usually love birthday parties

Tell me what's wrong, what is it, tell me why you're so scared??

Stop embarrassing me/being such a baby/ making such a fuss

Oh no, I think you have anxiety like
me/your dad/sist/aunt/friend, etc.

I wish I could help you get rid of your anxiety,
but I just don't know how

You're so SHY aren't you. You're the shy one in the family
and your sister is the confident one

I can see you're nervous and I want to help
you stop being so nervous

I'm going to take you to see X so that they can make you better

Phrases that may be helpful TO say:

I can see you're really scared/anxious. I get it.
Everyone has anxious thinking sometimes

Where can you feel it in your body?

I know it feels yucky, but I know you can handle it.
You can do hard things

These feelings will pass on, I promise you won't feel like this forever

You're totally safe. I'm going to stay with you until the feelings pass

It's okay to be anxious, it's normal to be anxious. I get anxious too

Underneath your anxious thinking, nothing has changed
—you're still you, you're still perfect

How about we go for a walk around the block
before we go into the party?

I totally trust that this will pass and when you're ready you will do it

[N.B. The phrases listed here are not meant to be learnt and repeated - and they will only 'work' if they come from a true place of heart. They have been included here to give you a flavour of the kind of approach that could potentially be unhelpful/helpful to your child.]

How to help after the moment (when your child is calm and back to their wellbeing)

Helping our children with anxiety is not about sitting them down and having a one-off conversation about it. It's most effective if it comes from our deep understanding of how the mind works and how to approach our own fears and anxieties—because our kids always pick up on the feeling within us much more than what we specifically say. They know at once if we're worried about something or consider it a problem and will join us in the exact same vibe. This is why I always prefer to work with parents rather than children. It's my experience that once the parent relaxes and learns how to handle themselves and their own anxious thinking, the effect on the child is dramatic.

The best way to teach our kids is always via modelling and living our own understanding. As we do this, we tend to find that helpful conversations and insights arise naturally and organically, and it's in these moments that our children are most likely to hear and be affected by what we are saying. My experience is that if there's even the slightest inkling of 'lecture mode' they tend to immediately close down and become completely deaf! So please know that what I've set out below are pointers and suggestions only. The more natural and authentic and 'you' flavoured you can be the better!

Share your own stories and experiences of seeing where our feelings come from. For example, notice times when you respond to the exact same situation or experience differently and share this with your child:

Tell them about times you've had or are having anxious thinking and what that was like for you. Often kids are amazed to hear that the adults in their life experience the same flow and variety of thinking as they do and are just as susceptible to anxiety and fears. Explain how you've come to see now that thinking is just energy taking form (or feeling real) in the moment and that it's always in flow and changing shape. In the same way that dark clouds always pass by (eventually) and we can see the sun again (because it never went anywhere, it was always still there behind the clouds—just as our light and wellbeing always is).

See if you can identify situations when your child is encountering the exact same situation as a sibling or a friend, but the experiences of each are very different because of their unique perspective. For example, when you visit a farm, your child is excited to feed the goats but her friend is terrified. Explain that your child is wearing 'goats are cute' glasses whereas her friend is wearing 'goats are scary' glasses. Point out that although these are the glasses they have on today, these can be whipped off and swapped or changed in any moment.

Even though we often like to think we can predict the future—"I hate goats and always will so I KNOW I'll be scared"—this is not in fact how it works. One thing that can be particularly helpful is to point them to specific situations where you notice this has happened—for example, "Do you remember last time we went to the reptile zoo you were terrified to go near the boa constrictor, and yet look at you now touching one!"

Another nice way to explain the temporary nature of feelings is to explain that they're like bubbles; they look pretty solid from the outside, but if you gently touch them they pop and disappear. And with feelings, just like with bubbles, there's no need to actively pop them; if you watch you'll notice how they eventually pop on their own. So, if feelings are this short-lived and fleeting, there's no need to take them so seriously or to think that they mean anything real about us.

If feelings are as gentle as bubbles, this means that however real and 3D and solid they look, they can't actually hurt us permanently. Yes, they can feel uncomfortable and sometimes very painful, BUT we can always handle it—it's built into the design of human beings to do so.

Do whatever makes sense to you to keep pointing them back to what's underneath the bubbles: who they really are when they're not caught up in anxious or upset thinking. See if you can identify the times when they seem to be most easily in this place. For some children it's when they're engaged in cartwheeling around the garden, for some it's swimming, and for some it's when they're curled up in their bed with their favourite comforter. Remind them that this sense of peace and wellbeing and flow they have when they're in this place is their true nature and is always there underneath the bubbles—even when it doesn't seem like it.

Explain to them that if they are feeling stuck or upset or not sure what to do, that this place of quiet underneath the bubbles is the best place to look. This calm place within them is where their light is' and where they can find all the answers they need. And that it's always best to wait until they are in this place to make a decision about something or to work out how they really feel.

Otherwise the bubbles can distract from discovering what's truly right for them.

AHHHHH
hhhhhh
gggggg

Catlin

I HATE you.
There is NO WAY
you are coming
to my party

Icant believe you
told her. I NEVER
want to see you
again.

I SHOULD SLEEP ON IT
THEN DECIDE

IN THE MORNING WHAT TO DO...

Finally, try to avoid putting your kids into fixed boxes, and using words like

'shy'   'retiring'   anxious'

in their hearing—or even not in their hearing if you can help it. Our children are deeply attuned to us and once given a label like this it can be very hard for them to shake and not unconsciously live up to. I strongly believe it to be the case that **our children become what we believe of them** and that there is deep truth in the saying that 'what we see is what we get'. The more we look towards our children's wholeness, light, resilience, and strengths, the more we draw this out of them. I'm not really clear about exactly why this is, but I know for sure the truth of it.

Summary

"*If you could perceive reality as it really is, you would be shocked by its colorless, odorless, tasteless silence. Outside your brain, there is just energy and matter. Over millions of years of evolution, the human brain has become adept at turning this energy and matter into a rich sensory experience of being in the world.*"

David Eagleman (neuroscientist), 2015

We are much more the same than we are different; we are all of the same energy of the universe, we all have the same light and divine spark within that never goes away, *no matter* our outward circumstances, history, or trauma.

What can obscure this is the power of THOUGHT taking form in the moment, and being brought to life so vividly through our senses that it feels completely real, permanent, and personal. But it is not; our reality is being *created* within us, moment-to-moment.

Anxious, fearful feelings come directly from anxious, fearful thoughts. Our experience of anxiety is always created internally, and not from anything happening outside of us.

Our thinking is constantly in flux and fresh thoughts and ideas can arrive at any moment. This is why we can encounter the exact same situation but on different occasions have a very varied experience of it; the meaning we make of the situation depends on our in-the-moment thinking.

Painful, uncomfortable feelings are our guides, our *friends*. They are a reminder that we have gone off-track and have got caught up in taking seriously thinking that is not in alignment with who we really are.
Knowing this allows us to be okay with these feelings and to simply allow them to pass through. It frees us from automatically identifying with them and taking them personally - and frees us from being afraid of any thought or feeling that may arrive.

No matter how stormy the thinking is or how broken we may feel, we NEVER actually are. Our inner light is always still there and contains all the wisdom, peace, resilience, love, and contentment we can ever need. Understanding that this is the way it works for all humans, 100% of the time—no exceptions—allows us to show up to our children from a much less fearful place. We can start to profoundly trust that, whatever happens, they (and we) can handle it, because they are quite literally designed to do so.

Clouds of Light

They look so small and frail
but they are so great and magnificent.
They are born of the same womb
that birthed the cosmos
and knitted together the galaxies.

If you could see them as they truly are,
you would be astounded.
You would see not little children,
but dancing clouds of light,
energy in motion,
swimming in an ocean of love.

They are so much more
than what you see.
As are you.

Life can seem mundane.
But it is not.
Children can seem ordinary,
and troublesome,
and fragile.
But they are not.
You may feel alone,
and separated,
and powerless.

But you are not.

William Martin

Final Thoughts

I wrote this book for that child I describe in the *Preface*, the one who was 'me' and yet from where I sit now seems like an entirely different, unrelated person. But as strange as it may sound, if I could go back, I wouldn't change one jot of her experience. Because I know for sure that if I did, I wouldn't have been compelled to search for answers, to help others, or write this book. It's also the case that I am genuinely devoid of any kind of regret or resentment. I have wonderful, loving parents and family and I hold not one shred of blame. Knowing what I do now, I can clearly see how all of that child's pain was innocently—*so* innocently— self-created. As the saying goes, *if she'd known better, she would have done better,* and it's very clear to me that she and everyone around her were doing the very best they could with what they knew at the time.

But it's now the case, of course, that our understanding has evolved and we do know better. And given that there is no doubt that our planet is becoming increasingly troubled, I feel more strongly than ever about raising children who are unburdened, and who don't have to spend their adult lives nursing or recovering from emotional wounds or in a permanent place of anger and defense. Now, more than ever, it looks vital to enable our children to stay in touch with and know who they really are, and grow into adults who are freed up to access and act on this wisdom for the good of the planet.

There is still a way to go in terms of sharing this perspective, and it's certainly not yet part of mainstream culture. So my heartfelt request is that if you've seen something here that looks like truth, that looks helpful, please play your part in sharing too. Whether it's this book, other copies of this book, any of the many, many wonderful resources listed on page 63, or via your own words or coaching—just sharing with one other person can create a ripple effect of unlimited potential transformation.

And of course, as I have mentioned already, one of the most effective ways to share is to simply LIVE what you see, and you will find that people cannot help but be touched by how you show up and become curious. In the wonderfully simple words of Sydney Banks:

"Concentrate on yourself.
Whatever you are, is all you can give away. That's very simple.
You open your wallet, you have a dollar; that's all you can give away.
You open your mind and it's full of anger, hate and distrust, sadness;
that's all you can give away.
But if your mind's full of love, that's what you can give."

Resources

If you are interested in deepening your understanding or exploring further what is shared here through personal, couple or family coaching, please contact me at:

nicola@heartparenting.com

or via Instagram at www.instagram.com/drnicolafarr/

I'm happy to discuss the possibility of working together or to refer you to one of many other brilliant coaches in this field who may be a good fit.

And here is a selection of just some of the resources that have had a significant impact on me and many of my clients:

Books about Parenting:

Being Human by Dr. Amy Johnson (Amy Johnson, 2013)
Parenting from the Heart by Jack Pransky (CCB Publishing, 1997)

Books specifically for children/youth:

The Spark Inside by Ami Chen Mills-Naim (Partners Publishing & Lone Pine Media Productions, 2016)
Inside Out Izzy by Angela Mastwijk (Sunsureness, 2014)
Do You Want to Know a Secret by Marie Arymar (Marie Arymar, 2018)
What is a Thought (A Thought is a Lot) by Jack Pransky and Amy Kahofer (Social Thinking Publishing)
What is Wisdom (and Where Do I Find It)? by Jack Pransky and Amy Kahofer (Amazon KDP)

Other Books :

The Missing Link: Reflections on Philosophy and Spirit by Sydney Banks (Lone Pine Publishing, 1989)

The Enlightened Gardener by Sydney Banks (Lone Pine Publishing, 2005)

The Little Book of Big Change by Dr. Amy Johnson (New Harbinger, 2016)

One Thought Changes Everything by Mara Gleason (CreateSpace, 2017)

The Inside-Out Revolution by Michael Neil (Hay House, 2013)

Results by Jamie Smart (Capstone, 2016)

Clarity by Jamie Smart (Wiley, 2013)

Coming Home by Dicken Bettinger and Natasha Swerdloff (CreateSpace, 2016)

Somebody Should Have Told Us by Jack Pransky (CCB Publishing, 2011)

Modello: A story of Hope for the Inner-City and Beyond by Jack Pransky (CCB Publishing, 1998)

The Relationship Handbook by George S. Pransky (Pransky & Associates, 2017)

Nuggets of Wisdom by Elsie Spittle (CreateSpace, 2016)

Beyond Imagination by Elsie Spittle (CreateSpace, 2013)

Island of Knowledge by Linda Quiring (CCB Publishing, 2015)

Fearproof Your Life: How to Thrive in a World Addicted to Fear by Joseph Bailey (Conari Press, 2007)

Victim of Thought: Seeing Through the Illusion of Anxiety by Jill Whalen (Jill Whalen, 2017)

Recovery From Within: A Mother and Daughter's Journey Through Anorexia by Rebecca Perkins and Beatrice Arscott (Rebecca Perkins and Beatrice Arscott, 2018)

Exquisite Mind: How a New Paradigm Transformed my Life…and is Sweeping the World by Terry Rubenstein (MX Publishing, 2016)

A Little Peace of Mind: The Revolutionary Solution for Freedom from Anxiety, Panic Attacks and Stress by Nicola Bird (Hay House, 2019)

Turning Stress on its Head by Dr Rani Bora

The Brain: The Story of You by David Eagleman (Random House, 2015)

State of Mind in the Classroom by Ami Chen Mills-Naim and Dr Roger C. Mills (Command Performance Language, 2016)

Websites:

Links to other Sydney Banks books, recordings and videos at

http://www.sydneybanks.org/

Dr Bill Pettit

https://thedrspettit.com/about-bill/

and links to his "Stories of Hope" podcast series about working with clients with a huge range of mental health issues at

https://thedrspettit.com/resources/

www.threeprinciplesmovies.com

www.three-principles.com/3p-reflections-essays

Dr Nicola Farr

Nicola Farr, PhD, is a coach, psychologist, writer, wife, mother of three, and ex-chronic anxiety and bulimia sufferer. She has devoted her academic and working life to supporting children and families—through research, intensive one-to-one work, and group intervention projects in a variety of settings, such as at-risk youth, young carers, and children with special needs.

Since having her three children she has worked in private practice and uniquely integrated her background and experience with a groundbreaking new approach to understanding the human condition. She is greatly privileged to support individuals and couples to come awake to the wisdom and light within themselves and their children, and to free them up to have more harmonious and joyful relationships and family lives.

heartparenting.com

Hannah Broadway

Hannah Broadway is an illustrator and designer. She has been working as an illustrator for over a decade, with a range of clients from the NHS to Nike, Bristol University to Bloomsbury Publishing. She has illustrated picture books, designed t-shirts and produced murals for hospitals. She sells a range of print and cards that celebrate her love of the little things in life-- and she knows just how lucky she is to do a job she loves!

Hannah lives in Bristol with her husband, little girl & 2 cats. She is learning to grow vegetables, is trying to get better at cycling up hills, and she continues to enjoy making it up as she goes along!

hannahbroadway.com

CPSIA information can be obtained
at www.ICGtesting.com
Printed in the USA
BVHW020024191121
621929BV00019BA/613